Sign up to our newsletter to
be the first to hear about new
releases, offers and more at...
www.pippapage.com

ISBN: 978-1-913467-42-5

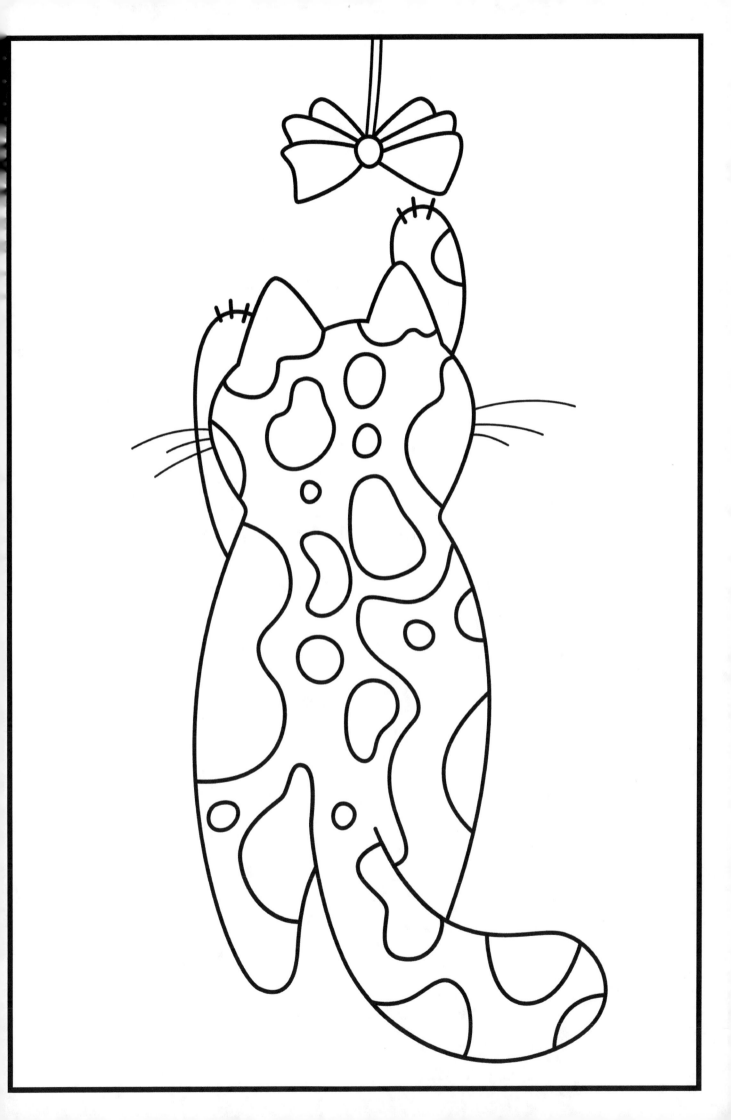

Thank you for purchasing our book.
Reviews on Amazon are really important to us and help others discover our artwork. We would really appreciate your feedback so please find a moment to share your thoughts by visiting this book on Amazon, scroll to customer reviews and leave your comments.

Thank you.

The Pippa Page collection represents a collective of independent artists & illustrators from around the world assembling a beautiful and diverse range of coloring pages.

Sign up to our newsletter to be the first to hear about new releases, offers and more at...

www.pippapage.com